So you want to Change your Church

A journey of faith
that could end up
changing the world

TIM RANDOLPH

So, You Wawnt to Change Your Church
A Journey of Faith that Could End of Changing the World

by Tim Randolph

ISBN: 978-0-9845366-9-6
© 2016 Tim Randolph

Pubished by Austin Brothers Publishing
Fort Worth, TX

www.austinbrotherspublishing.com

Austin Brothers Publishing
www.austinbrotherspublishing.com

Printed in the United States - 2016

ACKNOWLEDGEMENTS

Every book needs the eyes and the minds of a team of folks in order to make it enjoyable and useful. This present offering is no different. Through the years, those faithful saints who have allowed me to come alongside them in their church/ life journey have contributed to all that herein follows. Others have more directly helped this actual book come into being.

To the staff and friends at the International Mission Board and the Baptist General Convention of Texas who generously shared their lives and their best thoughts with me, and afforded me some unimaginable training opportunities.

To the churches that eagerly, early in the process, allowed me to try an experiment with them to see what works in helping churches to change.

To the leaders of the Waco Regional Baptist Association who have patiently and thoughtfully participated in the development of the WRBA Church Strengthening Process.

To those who helped with the editing of this book.

My sincerest thanks.

CONTENTS

Suggestions for the use of this book   1

Preface   5

Why would you want to change your church?   9

Where do you start?   15

How does a church rediscover its mission?   23

What is important to your church?   31

What would your church look like if it succeeded?   37

What do you need to do in the next five years?   45

What barriers can you expect?   53

Why should you persevere?   65

What else must you consider?   71

The Author   77

SUGGESTIONS FOR THE USE OF THIS BOOK

This book was written for both group and individual use. If you are reading this as an individual, you should plan to read one chapter each day, and take the time to write out your answers to the questions at the end of each chapter. Working through the questions may well be the most beneficial part of this experience.

If you are leading a group through this book, the members should each read the chapter and answer the questions on their own before coming to the meeting of the group. It would be ideal if the group could convene once a week for nine consecutive weeks. The leader should read the entire book before beginning the journey with a group.

The meetings should consist of prayer, one person bringing a concise summary of the contents of the chapter, and then extended conversation through the questions. The leader of the group should be particularly sensitive to helping the group:

- Be honest.
- Respect other members of the congregation who are not presently in the group.
- Keep the conversation focused on *what do you need to do to positively change our church?*
- Maintain a summary written record of the conclusions of your group, and share those appropriately with the leadership of your church.

If you are leading your church through this book, you are probably working with a consultant from your Association or district. In the Waco Regional Baptist Association, we offer our member congregations the option of participating with a trained staff person as a part of the Waco Regional Baptist Association Church Strengthening Process. Allow your consultant to help shape the experience for your church.

One way to use this book for the entire congregation is to organize two town hall style meetings for the congregation. The first town hall meeting would be to launch this project as a process to strengthen your church. During this first town hall meeting, a leader would give an overview of the book and of the church strengthening process that is beginning. Small groups, gathered around tables, then would be given the preface and asked to read it and the questions at the end of the preface. Time is taken to discuss in the small groups around the tables. After ample time for discussion, one representative from each table would share a summary of what their table said. This first town hall meeting should focus on prayer, seeking the Lord's leadership through the entire process.

The second town hall meeting could be when all of the small groups have finished reading and discussing the entire book. Again, spokespersons from the groups would summarize major areas of new insights, discoveries, and recommendations.

Chapter 9 deals with the particularly sensitive issue of the church leadership. The obvious delicate nature of this issue might quickly convince you to not want to discuss this topic. Here is a suggestion to overcome that fear. Have the individual members read and pray through that chapter by themselves, and then appoint a trusted lay leader (or outside consultant), to be available to the members to receive their thoughts and answers to the questions at the end of that particular chapter.

Members might communicate their thoughts in person, or by email, or by an anonymous survey. Then the trusted lay leader needs to meet with the Senior Pastor and convey the summary of the comments he or she has received. These comments need to be considered prayerfully and seriously by the pastor and other elders or senior leaders of the congregation. If it appears that changes in the area of pastoral staff need to happen, then the maturity and grace and courage of all of the leaders will be tested on this point. I have seen churches and pastors come to a graceful and mutual understanding that a change needs to be made. In each instance, this has been the fruit of patient, prayerful, and courageous conversations over a period of months. In these few cases, the church and pastor have been able to navigate the transition without damaging each other significantly.

PREFACE

This book was written to give church members and leaders a map with practical markers to empower them to positively change their church. The flow of the book follows the chronological steps in the Waco Regional Baptist Association's Church Strengthening Process. It can be used by any church member or leader as a guide for personal renewal, and then secondarily to help that member participate in a process that will give their church new strength, focus, and increased effectiveness in accomplishing its mission.

There are many assumptions and beliefs behind this book that cannot be fully articulated here, but they deserve at least a brief mention.

The church is both an organism and an organization. There is a mysterious life through the presence of the Holy Spirit in the church that prevents it from being just another not-for-profit organization. The local church is both divine and human. We readily see the humanity of the local church. The divine element requires equal attention when we speak of strengthening or changing a church. What can possibly help a church if it is not soaked in prayer, faith, integrity, hope, and love? The Apostle Paul captured this reality when he said, "Now you are the body of Christ, and each one of you is a part of it."

Churches regularly need renewal and strengthening. As living entities, they are subject to the same pitfalls as all other human organizations: mission drift, the normal life cycle of an organization, status quo in the face of changing communities, lethal leaders, misalignment of values and resources, and complacency experienced as mediocrity. Churches can be forced to adapt through changes in leadership, disaster (like a fire or flood), or dramatic growth (or decline) in the community. This book is written with the conviction that churches ought to intentionally pursue positive change regularly. That is probably why you are reading these pages, because you sense it is time to get your church moving forward in a positive direction.

Intentional change comes to a church through conversation; it cannot effectively be accomplished by mere fiat or decree, even though there must be a leader to initiate and guide that conversation. A church is a voluntary organization with relatively few paid employees. Most of the real change is accomplished by consensus derived from a thoughtful dialogue over a span of time between those who are invested in its future. That conversation must include the Lord! After all, He is the chief stakeholder in any church that bears and proclaims His name. For that reason, the entire church must be able to participate in the conversation about its future. Also, real, productive conversations happen over a period of time, not just in one day.

The context and the membership of every congregation are unique in terms of their perspective, focus, and culture. Churches resist a *franchise* approach. A conversation is needed to shape how that unique church will function effectively in its current environment.

Strengthening any organism implies change and work. You cannot possibly think of strengthening your physical body without spending both time and energy. If you are reading this book with the hopes of changing your church for the better, you also have to assume that it will cost you significant time and energy.

Questions for Conversation

- *How invested are you in the future of your church?*

- *What is at stake in this conversation?*

- *How many other members and leaders are convinced that things need to change?*

Notes

WHY WOULD YOU WANT TO CHANGE YOUR CHURCH?

So you want to change your church? Congratulations! That implies that (1) you value your church enough to stay with it and attempt to make it better, and (2) you feel like your church is not living up to its full potential, yet. You have spotted some deficiencies and believe there is still hope. Maybe you have zeroed in on the *problem* and perhaps you have even personified that problem by sticking it onto one person or one group—very often the pastor.

Could I urge two words of caution upon you? (1) Don't be overly quick in identifying the cause of the ills that you see in your church. Churches are very complex organisms. They are similar to our physical bodies. I have a pain sometimes in my side that my doctor tells me is because of a problem in my hip. (2) Don't forget to start with yourself. Jesus' analogy of the log and the speck in the eye reminds us of our tendency to blindness in regard to ourselves, and our pickiness in regard to others.

So let's begin with an understanding of why your church could probably use some improvements. The Church Life Cycle illustrates the natural progression of a church through the years.

Any church begins with a vision in the heart of a leader or a small group of believers. Most churches have nothing else other than vision when they start. They do not have many leaders, or programs, or resources (buildings & budgets). They have a gleaming desire to gather and disciple a certain people group, and eventually to transform some community with the good news of Jesus.

I borrowed the following drawing from the Church Life Plus Notebook produced by the Baptist General Convention of Texas. (This drawing is used with permission from the authors.) It traces the church life-cycle with these four elements: Vision, Leadership, Programs, and Resources. Where the letters are capitalized (VLPR), those elements are predominant and functional. Where the letters are lower case, they represent the fact that the elements are either missing or very weak. The cycle can occur over a period of 50 years or less. This drawing doesn't take into account the changing community around the church.

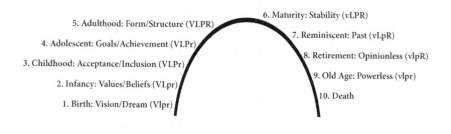

5. Adulthood: Form/Structure (VLPR)

6. Maturity: Stability (vLPR)

4. Adolescent: Goals/Achievement (VLPr)

7. Reminiscent: Past (vLpR)

3. Childhood: Acceptance/Inclusion (VLPr)

8. Retirement: Opinionless (vlpR)

2. Infancy: Values/Beliefs (VLpr)

9. Old Age: Powerless (vlpr)

1. Birth: Vision/Dream (Vlpr)

10. Death

V = Vision   L = Leadership   P = Programs   R = Resources

When the letter is uppercase, it is a defining and strong characteristic of the church.
When it is lowercase, the characteristic is either missing or weak.

If your church is in the period of productivity (at the top of the curve), it is definitely time to talk about the future. As a church slides into decline, the resources are the last element to vanish. Very often, as the congregation senses it is losing ground, the mission of the group subtly changes to *let's preserve the resources* (the buildings & budget). At some point, the church loses the option to dream of a new future and to change. That church will die.

Renewal can begin in unusual places. I was invited as a college student to lead the youth group in a small church in west Texas during a Lay Renewal Weekend. During the Saturday night session, the dozen youth sat in a circle and read together from 1 John 4. We read verses 7 and 8 in unison, "Dear friends, let us love one another, for love comes from God. Everyone who loves has been born of God and knows God. Whoever does not love does not know God, because God is love." (NIV)

A dead silence came over the whole group. After some difficult moments, one young teenager began to sob and said, "I have never told my adoptive parents that I love them."

After some more talking and prayer, she left the circle and found a telephone. She called the couple that had adopted her as a little girl, and she asked them to forgive her for her unloving spirit, and told them for the first time that she loved them. Those parents immediately came to the church, found their daughter, embraced her, and wept together. I don't really know what happened during the rest of that night, but I do remember that by the next morning, the church house was full, and at the conclusion of the service, more people were waiting in the aisles to make a public recommitment of their life to Christ than were remaining in their pews. The church that was literally at the edge of dying had come to life because one teenager came to grips with what she needed to do to obey Jesus, and she did it.

Questions for conversation

- *Where is your church right now in the church life cycle? How do you know that?*

- *Have you already noticed people attempting to pin the blame on an individual or a group? How productive has that been toward producing a stronger, healthier church?*

- *Where are you personally in your journey with the Lord?*

    Passionate, but possibly ignorant?
    Growing and fruitful?
    Faithful, but bored?
    Faultfinding and jaded?
    Checked out?

- *What do you need to experience personal renewal in your relationship with the Lord?*

- *What is keeping you back?*

NOTES

WHERE DO YOU START?

A quick inventory of our conversations betrays who owns the church. Often, the church is referred to as *pastor so and so's church*, or this is *my church*. When the question is posed, "Who really runs your church?" the answers vary from the deacons or elders to a few select people who bother to show up at church conference meetings. Only when we bring out the Bible and put on our spiritual language do we begin to speak of the church as belonging to Jesus. He purchased it with His death on the cross. He anointed it with His Holy Spirit as the church burst across the globe in the first century. The truth is that any effort to strengthen or renew a church without establishing this reality as the cornerstone of everything else will be a futile waste of energy.

I have interviewed many church and denomination-al leaders, and one common observation about effective church leaders and vibrant church ministries is that they have spiritual vitality. Effective church leaders walk with God, and they love the Lord above all else. The worship services are *alive* precisely because those who are shap-ing the service are consistently and intentionally seeking to live in God's presence and to serve Him with all they possess. Therefore, before we even start the conversation about strategy, your community, and strengths and weak-nesses, we must come face to face with the most basic question: "How is your walk with God?"

You may have picked up this book thinking, "Good, now I will learn how to get those people to listen to me and make the church like I think it ought to be."

If that was your thought, then this book will be a big disappointment for you. True spiritual renewal in your church depends upon you becoming renewed in your walk with Christ, and in your relationship to your fellow church members. But what does a spiritually renewed person look like? How do you know the measure of your walk with God and your walk with your fellow believers? Some (mistaken-ly) look for emotional fervor or experiences. Others base their self-evaluation of their nearness to God on the suc-cess of their particular ministry. The New Testament gives both teachings and portrayals of spiritually alive believers.

Let me distill what I have learned about spiritual vital-ity by looking at the example of early believers in the New

Testament. (Note that this list only hits high points. The area is rich for deep study, and I encourage you to pursue such a study.)

A spiritually alive believer...

- Yearns to be in the presence of Jesus daily. No prior commitment or long-standing habit or unexpected interruption keeps a thirsty person from pursuing water. Likewise, a spiritually-alive Christian finds ways to spend quality time with Jesus each day, because that is the focus, source, purpose, and most satisfying thing in life.

- Delights to obey Jesus, and regularly seeks to understand more of what Jesus taught. The genuine pursuit of Christ regularly challenges our contemporary lifestyle and cultural norms. It is an understatement to say that many facets of our culture run contrary to obeying Jesus. This produces a continual struggle in the life of the awakened Christian.

- Displays a quietness and humility that could only be a result of the fruit of the Spirit (as found in Galatians 5:22-23). Sometimes, the more spiritually-alive are the least aware of their own spiritual health because they are continually reflecting upon and comparing themselves with the Savior.

- Seeks the welfare of others. Through times of conflict, they seek reconciliation. Through times of loss and pain, they seek to comfort. Through times of failure, they seek restitution and restoration. The believer who is walking with Christ has no difficulty in seeing and identifying Christ in the other person, because He is a familiar face and voice.

Although this cannot possibly be an exhaustive list of measures of spiritual vitality, these few points often are enough get us started in the right direction. Go back over this list of symptoms of spiritual vitality, and place in the column beside each bullet point a number between 1 and 5 to indicate how well you believe those words describe your current behavior (1 = hardly describes me at all, and 5 = describes me perfectly). If you are scoring in the 1 or 2 range, you might want to reflect on what changes you need to make in your own spiritual life.

The other aspect of personal spiritual renewal that will gradually influence your church is your relationships with fellow church members. Jesus made it clear that loving Him and loving our brother are inseparable (1 John 4:7-21). Only the deceived can imagine that they have a great relationship with Jesus while at the same time they are apathetic about their relationship with fellow believers. There is an old joke about a pastor who said, "I love being a pastor; it's the people I can't stand!" The irony of that statement stands in stark contrast to Jesus' words about love being the quality that would identify us as His followers.

So, you want to change your church? Where do you start? Through renewing your own living, breathing, walking, talking, daily relationship with Jesus and with your fellow church members.

It starts with me:

Jackson and Judy had been members of their open-country Baptist Church for most of their lives. Now, in their retirement years, they were heartbroken as they watched their church get torn into pieces through harsh fundamentalism. A new pastor had come to power, and was liberally using the pulpit to ridicule and bully those who disagreed with his teachings. The withering diatribes caused many to simply leave and find somewhere else to worship.

Judy and Jackson sat in my office with tears streaming down their faces as they explained what seemed like a hopeless situation. They missed their church family. They missed having great times of worship. As we visited about options available to them, they concluded that even though they were (now) in the minority, that they would not give up. They would persevere in their church no matter what. They also determined to be Christian about their conduct and their attitudes.

So they sat on the front row, Sunday after Sunday, praying for their church, and for their church family. The pastor tried every way he could to get them to leave. Finally, in an act of desperation, the pastor announced that he and his loyal followers were going to take over an abandoned church building some five miles away and start a new church. At that, Jackson and Judy patiently went around and lovingly invited their neighbors and friends back to church. They found a seminary student to be their pastor, and again saw their church flourish with new life.

Questions for conversation:

- *If everyone in your church prayed and worshiped as you do, would your church truly be alive?*

- *Name some recent examples of how your effort to obey the teachings of Jesus led you into conflict with the expectations and norms of the rest of the world.*

- *What broken or strained relationships need to be mended in order for you to honestly say, "I am at peace with all my fellow church members?"*

- *Is there someone about whom you have been privately critical, but in their presence you are completely nice?*

- *Which aspects of the fruit of abiding in the Spirit (from Galatians 5:22-23) are easily seen in your life? Which ones are more difficult to see?*

- *Who acts and talks like they own the church you attend? Do you ever participate in that kind of talk? How would the decisions made at your church be changed if* every motion began with the phrase, "because Jesus is the head of this church, we propose the following..."?

- Every church is a living organism. As such, they are never the same. Last year's church isn't the same as this year's church. A church is subject to spurts of growth, periods of decline, times of renewal, and catastrophic loss. How would you describe the health and vitality of your church right now? How is your life wrapped up in that same condition?

- What do you need to do differently over the next week in order to contribute to your church's healthy future?

NOTES

HOW DOES A CHURCH REDISCOVER ITS MISSION?

Groups of people frequently suffer from an inability to attain and maintain a sharp focus on what it is that they are collectively trying to accomplish. Whether we are watching a group of 5 year-olds trying to play T-Ball, or sitting in on a youth committee meeting trying to plan the events and ministry programs for the next year, we realize that groups are constantly under pressure to get distracted. This is simply a manifestation of our creative and adaptive abilities. Churches frequently forget why they exist. We get caught up in solving the latest problem or preventing the next one, and we forget to check the compass or the horizon and ask ourselves, "Are we headed in the right direction?" and "What is the right direction?"

As a church begins to talk about its future, the first question that it must answer is "Why does this church exist?" The answer to that question will be foundational to all other questions in this effort to focus and energize the church toward a vibrant future.

The importance of this question is betrayed by its simplicity. Many church leaders want to dismiss it by referring to a favorite verse of Scripture such as the Great Commission, and then move on to the details of what are we going to do next year. When a church hurries past this point, it assumes that everyone in the congregation already knows the answer to that question, and everyone already agrees on the same answer. Both of these assumptions are probably wrong.

Part of the struggle here is due to the fact that the answer to that question, "Why does this church exist?" is both universal and particular. A church's purpose is universal in the sense that it shares much of its purpose for existence with all churches of all cultures throughout history. But it is particular because this church exists in a unique community at a unique time in history.

So, how does a church rediscover and articulate its sense of purpose? The conversation must include all of the constituents of the church for whom the success of the church matters. These constituents include Jesus, the owner and head of the church; the church staff and leaders; both the long-time members and the new members; the community around the church; and all of the groups of its members. It is interesting to ask some people who are very different from yourself about why this church should continue to exist. A member of the youth group tends to answer differently than a member of the senior adults.

The key here is to realize that we all tend to approach the church from the perspective that it exists to meet some of my needs. If my needs are friendship and companions for the final chapters of life, then that easily becomes the reason for the church's existence.

In order to rediscover the church's complete mission, we must look at it from several different angles. What does Jesus expect from the church? What does the community expect/need from the church? What do the children need the church to do? What do the "good" people in the community need from the church? What do the "bad" people need the church to be? How about the broken and hurting people? When we see the church's purpose from these various perspectives, we realize how challenging it is to articulate the church's mission in a simple sentence.

That conversation is very rewarding, however, in that it helps us all appreciate the church's unique role in history and in our lives. There is no other organization designed by God to fulfill the mission of the church. There are lots of non-profit organizations that do good things, but none of them hold as their mission the comprehensive redemptive mission of the church.

There are a few questions that can facilitate this conversation about the mission of the church. Here are some of my favorites: If this church building were to be destroyed, and the members were forced to dissipate and never to gather together again,

- What would you miss?
- What would the people in this neighborhood miss?
- How would the future of this community be affected?

Here is another intriguing question that frequently helps people articulate the purpose of the church: "Can you think of any Scripture passages that talk about what a church is supposed to do?"

You may think there are only one or two Scriptures that closely speak to the mission of the church, but you will probably be surprised when you hear the answers given by other church members. Listen carefully to the others as they answer these questions. What does the diversity of opinions tell you?

Your church's mission statement should be able to focus all of the conversations about the future including budget, staffing, programming and calendar planning. The mission statement should be simple enough that active members can remember and recite it easily.

I used to think that the question, "Why does this church exist?" was an easy question until I began asking church leaders and listening to their answers. Even within the same church, I have been surprised by the diversity of the answers that key leaders offer. In one First Baptist Church, a sincere deacon announced, "That is easy! The church exists for evangelism!" He offered that answer with such a definitive and authoritative tone of voice that a long silence followed from his fellow committee members.

In order to help them move forward, I offered, "So that means bringing people to trust in Jesus, right?" His response was affirmative.

I then offered, "So when a church leads a nine-year-old boy to trust Jesus, the church has nothing more to do with that boy?"

"Of course not", the man answered.

I then asked if the church's mission included meeting the needs of its senior adult members. The rest of the meeting opened up to exploring the other facets of the purpose of the church.

Questions for conversation

- *If you were to write the church's mission statement just to accommodate people exactly like you, what would it say?*

- *What is missing?*

- *Has your church already tried to express its sense of mission in a single sentence? Can anyone remember it or find it?*

- *How would it impact the ministry plan for the coming year if the conversation began with the mission of the church?*

NOTES

WHAT IS IMPORTANT TO YOUR CHURCH?

I frequently introduce the concept of values by telling a fictitious story. Imagine that I own a 15-year-old car that is beat up, rusty, and worn out. If I take that car to the grocery store, and see a fellow shopper accidentally let his shopping cart slide into the door of my car, I might not get too upset. It wouldn't be the first dent in that door, and I would probably just shrug it off as "one more won't hurt."

Now change the picture just slightly, and this time it is the brand new Lexus that I worked three years to save for. I dreamed about buying this car, and on the way home from the showroom, I stop at the grocery store. Now my reaction to the careless jerk who let the cart ding into the door would probably be a little more energetic. Right?

Now change the situation once more. I'm at the grocery store parking lot, and instead of dinging my car with a shopping basket, a stranger reaches out and grabs the arm of my five-year-old son and starts to drag him away. NOW, I really respond. Right?

What is the difference? It is the value of that which is threatened that matters. Old car = low value. My own son = high value. We react to what matters to us, especially when what we love or cherish is threatened.

A church behaves much in the same way. A church collectively holds a list of values, and when those values are threatened, the church will react. No question. One of the problems with this conversation about values is that churches are often unconscious of their real values. They exist, and they motivate us, but we cannot label them clearly. Outsiders can often see them more clearly than insiders.

People join your values when they join your church. Church fights and splits frequently occur over a difference of values. Values are not easily changed. This booklet is intended to help a church discover the values that are already there, not to invent the values they wish they had. Values show up in every activity of a church.

So how can your congregation discover its real values?

Look inside your church. Your budget, the calendar, and the programming already tell you something about what is important to your church. Ask those outside of your church to give you their impressions of what your church is famous for in the community. Make a list, and then do a simple test that I call the "allergic reaction test." As you look at the list of possible values for your church, erase one item from the list, and then ask yourself if that element were to be removed, would it cause a riot in your church? Would your congregation break out in "hives"?

Some churches like to think that missions or ministry are a value to them, but the truth is that if it were removed, nothing about the church would change much. You will want to discover what the real values are, not the wished-for values. Your church's values are unique to your church. They define the identity of your church.

"We love to cook and eat!"

The Creekside Baptist Church is nestled in the northern part of the hill country in Texas. The church is located on a tiny asphalt county road. As the deacons and the pastor discussed their future, I asked them what they were really good at (as a church body). They laughingly offered that they could really put on good "feeds" (meaning dinners for guests). They didn't think that was much to brag about, but there we were sitting in a large new metal building with beautiful patios all around lined with picnic tables and a lovely new kitchen, it became very obvious that sharing meals together was hugely important to them.

They fed every family that had a funeral. They regularly had covered dish dinners for every holiday. They had smokers big enough to cook 30 briskets at once! Their money, their calendar, and their energy plainly indicated that fellowship meals were important to this rural congregation. I asked them how they could use this to help accomplish their mission. After some hard thought, they determined that they would rally everyone around three or four big events each year. Every member of the church could get involved by inviting everyone in their part of the county to the dinner. They would have a good program of music, fun, fellowship, preaching, and yes, eating a fine meal. They would then follow up with everyone who came out for the dinner with a personal visit, and an invitation to come back on Sunday and join them for church. Their church quickly doubled in size because they could identify what was important to them, and they capitalized on it.

Questions for conversation:

- *What do friendly outsiders frequently say about your church?*

- *What attracted you to join this church? Are those elements still present?*

- *If you had three million dollars given to your church, with the only condition that you had to spend it in the next 12 months, how do you think your church would spend it?*

- *What do those choices say about the values of your church?*

- *Are there any values you wish your church embraced, but it actually doesn't?*

NOTES

WHAT WOULD YOUR CHURCH LOOK LIKE IF IT SUCCEEDED?

Your church's mission is the answer to the question, "Why does this church exist?"

Your church's values answer the question, "What is important to us?"

Your church's vision statement will answer the question, "What would we look like if we succeeded?" More specifically, your vision will describe the kind of church you will have if you succeed at focusing on your mission and remaining loyal to your values. In a simplistic way, the Vision of the Church is simply this mathematical formula: Mission + Values = Vision.

I have seen churches that indicated that life in a small group was essential to spiritual growth. They thought that was so important that regular participation in a life group was a requirement for continuing in the membership of the church. As a result of honoring their values, they intentionally encouraged their church to meet all across the large city in hundreds of homes every week.

These exercises with words can be daunting and tiring. In fact, some doubt the value of forming statements about your vision and values. I would like to assert that if you cannot explain what it is you are trying to build, you will probably not get a lot of cooperation in building it. Neither will you be able to track from year to year whether you are actually making progress.

Can you imagine a couple who sets out to build their dream retirement home, but they cannot describe that "dream house" to the architect? The description of your future church should not focus on talking about numbers, but rather about images, qualities, characteristics, or behaviors of the church. If the resulting sentence fits nicely on the church sign out front, great, but it is more important that it communicates clearly the kind of church you believe God is calling you to be. Through prayer and thoughtful conversations, your congregation should be able to affirm this expression of your future as your understanding of God's will for your congregation in your lifetime.

"Google is not the answer"

I was working with a planning committee from a First Baptist Church and the evening was getting late. The committee members were exhausted, and I was trying to stimulate their thoughts towards a possible Vision Statement. One of the sharp ladies in the group grabbed her smart phone and Googled "Baptist Church Vision Statements" and gave the group a list of three or four samples that came up off of church web sites. She was so disappointed when I said "Google is not the answer."

The reason is that each church is unique. While we all share some sense of the same mission, our values are distinct, and the resulting church will be different from one community to another.

"The point of this," I explained, "is not a clever marketing logo, but to be able to describe the kind of church you are working to build."

One local church posted on their website the following introduction to their vision: "...our leadership team spent 18 months seeking input from leaders throughout the body of Christ..." It is not an easy or a quick task to put into words what you think God is calling you as a congregation to do.

As a leader for a local Baptist Association, I frequently see church leaders who are very busy. Church leaders today have meetings, visits to hospitals, funerals, phone calls, and seminars to attend. But sometimes there is a failure to connect the dots between what a church leader does with his/her time and the overall vision of the congregation.

One young pastor recently confessed to me that he had spent an entire day trying to help a homeless man. While that is a good thing to do, the blank look on his face told me he had no idea what that entire day had to do with his responsibility to lead the church to fulfill its mission, honor its values, and become the church God had called them to be. It is almost as if we begin with lots of activities, and then blindly hope that by working lots of hours and attending lots of meetings, we'll actually (or accidentally) stumble upon fulfilling our purpose as a church.

We avoid accountability in the church partly because we aren't sure what we should be held accountable for doing. We measure and count a few things like small group attendance, worship attendance, and offerings (can't forget that!), and assume that magically those numbers will tell us if we are on track on not. Are those numbers the ones that really matter at the end of a decade of ministry?

The vision of a church will end up defining the goals that your church chooses to focus upon for the next five years. If your vision is for a church that actively and personally ministers in multiple countries across the globe that will impact your budget, your staffing, your calendar, and even your prayer list. If your church envisions itself being a transforming people in the inner city, it will affect who you partner with, where you locate, and what kinds of leadership development you deploy.

It is not unlike the blueprint that an architect drafts of the building the client wants to build. In the moment, the blueprint is not the building. It is just words and lines on pieces of paper. But every contractor and worker can look at those words and understand what he/she needs to do in order to complete that building. Your church's vision should guide the energies of all of the leaders and members in such a clear way that they all know what they can contribute to the effort to build that kind of church.

Sometimes the vision comes in the form of the dream of the founding pastor. Other times it morphs over years into a collective agreement between the members of the kind of church all of them collectively want.

Pastor Charles came to meet me at my office from a distant state. He introduced himself as a life-long Baptist pastor who grew up in my community. He was nearing retirement and felt the Lord calling him to start a new church in this small county seat town. When I asked him what kind of church he wanted to start, without hesitation, he announced, "It is going to be the largest evangelical church in town with exciting contemporary worship that nurtures healthy Christian families." Further, he elaborated that they would only focus on five things: Exciting/relevant worship, cutting edge youth and children's ministries, family counseling, and home cell groups. He believed that if they could focus on those five things well, they would succeed. Guess what? In ten years, CCC was the largest church in town with great worship, children's, youth, cell groups, and counseling ministries. Everyone that joined the church knew exactly what kind of church they were joining, and therefore they knew how to contribute to make it possible. Most church experiences do not include such a crisp and sharp vision. It is not uncommon to visit a church and hear two or three different visions for the future. "We are going to be a missional church!" announces the pastor. The youth minister touts a hip and casual "come as you are" church, and the deacons discuss how to keep it a traditional county seat First Baptist Church. No wonder we end up nowhere. We haven't agreed on where we are going.

Questions for conversation

- *Can you remember a Vision Statement from any church? What is it that attracted you to that expression of calling?*

- *Who is responsible to cast the vision for the church? To formulate it? To hold it?*

- *Have you seen an instance when key leaders of a congregation had a different vision than the body of believers? How did that work out?*

- *On a scale of 1 (very fuzzy) to 5 (very clear), how clear is the vision of your congregation right now? What is lacking?*

NOTES

WHAT DO YOU NEED TO DO IN THE NEXT 5 YEARS?

At a Global Leadership Summit, Bill Hybels, pastor of Willow Creek Church, stated that we need to evaluate and re-think everything we are doing as a church at least every three years. Has your church been doing some of the same things the same exact way for the past 20 years?

Consider how much of our lives have changed because of changes in culture, changes in technology, and massive global migration in those same 20 years. Your community is not the same community that was there 20 years ago. The younger generations are living differently, moral standards have shifted radically. Churches are confronting new questions that it never dreamed of having to discuss. Even in your parents' wildest imagination, did they ever think that a request would have to go out on Sunday morning for people to silence their cell phones before the worship service started?

It is probably time to rethink some of the things your church is doing. Generally, we think of setting goals as finding new things that we are going to embrace, and new initiatives we are willing to undertake. I would like to suggest that a good prior step to setting new goals would be to list all of the programs, events, budget items and activities on a sheet of paper, and then to ask some very hard questions. How is this (event, program, budget item, etc.) helping us to accomplish our mission, honor our values and become the church we are called to be? To effectively embrace some new directions, most churches will need to modify or abandon some of the old things that have been consuming your energies and resources. To pretend otherwise is to assume that your committed people have unlimited money and time. We all know that is not true. Maybe the first step in goal setting should be to determine what you are not going to continue to do in the same way.

As a backdrop for the conversation about what your church should focus on during the next few years, you will want to have the opportunity to get everyone informed on what your church is already doing well. If your area of focus is the youth ministry, it would not be unusual for you to be unaware of what is happening in the area of preschool ministry, or in the overall budget of the church. This is a good moment to get curious and start those conversations.

What is going well in your church? What is ailing in your church? What is happening in the community around you that you consider your church field? Are there some threats or opportunities looming in your community?

Wise decisions are informed decisions. Most members possess small tidbits of valuable information, but rarely does one person possess all of those important answers. Town hall style meetings are a great way for the church to gather and think about what is happening, both inside and outside of the church. But town hall meetings can be a nightmare if done incorrectly. Here are some helpful tips to have a productive town hall meeting with a fairly large church body:

- Schedule the town hall meeting for an evening when members can dedicate two hours to a good, focused conversation. You might need to provide a light dinner in order for it to happen.
- Set the schedule and stick to it!
- Define the purpose of the discussion and the major question(s) that are expected to be answered ahead of time.
- Organize all participants into small groups of six or eight around tables in the fellowship hall and select a secretary and a spokesperson for each table. Provide markers and chart paper for the group

to record their thoughts. Please, avoid the "open mic" night in the worship center! The people who most often grab for the microphone are not usually the ones that the church needs to hear from. It is the quiet thoughtful members who often have a lot to say if given the opportunity.

- Ask one good question at a time, and let the small groups work at their tables for a limited period of time. At the conclusion of the small group time, have the spokesperson present a very succinct summary of what that group concluded. The moderator of the town hall meeting may summarize the major things that the church has spoken during this time.
- The information shared during this time should be channeled back to a task force or a committee that will then interpret and polish the findings for later presentation back to the whole church body.
- Dismiss on time.

Your church needs to identify what is happening inside and outside of the church. The issues that you find inside the church can be divided into strengths and weaknesses. The trends that you see outside of your church in the community can fall into the categories of opportunities or threats.

As the church grapples with the changes that have already occurred inside and outside of the body, ideas will begin to flow about potential goals for the future. A good planning process will yield a few really great goals that the whole membership can enthusiastically embrace and begin to pursue. The goals should probably express what your church could reasonably accomplish in five years (or less) if it tried to focus on that area of ministry. I like to use the common acronym "SMART" to describe goals that are useful to move a church forward.

A "SMART Goal" has these attributes:

Sensible. The goal makes sense for your church or for the group.

Measureable. The goal can be measured so that anyone can see when it is actually completed.

Attainable. You will want to set your church up to succeed.

Responsible. The goal is clear about who is responsible to carry out the goal.

Time-Stamped. There is a moment out there in the future when you hope to complete the goal.

Here are a few more bits of wisdom about goal setting in a church. Churches often overestimate what they can accomplish in one year, but underestimate what they can do in five years. Churches sometimes forget to evaluate what they are measuring, and as a result they keep measuring the same things that no longer relate to what they are trying to accomplish. As the goals are embraced by the congregation, someone needs to ask "who," "where," and "how" will the progress on this goal be measured?

A goal helps coordinate and energize our collective efforts towards a common thing. That is true to the degree to which we genuinely share that goal, and believe it to be worthwhile. We all grow more apathetic about fulfilling a goal that someone else wrote for us. It is important during this phase of the conversation about the future of your church that all of the primary stakeholders be able to participate freely in the discussion about what goals will guide us. Honest, open talk about what is needed, what is possible, and how motivated we are feeling about the issues at hand is critical to coming up with a successful plan.

I recently ate lunch with a pastor who was accused by some key church leaders of "not leading the church forward." After some question and answer time, the pastor said, "It became clear that the church body expected him to fulfill the plan they had approved five years before."

The pastor has been at this church for four years, and he had very little awareness that there was even a plan in place. He had no say in building the plan. Now everyone was frustrated. Churches are not exactly like businesses or corporations where the pyramid of power can hand out orders and expect them to be fulfilled simply because they are written. The real truth of the matter is that businesses and corporations do not function that way either. It takes an on-going dialogue between important stakeholders to establish what needs to be accomplished and how fast it can be done. Once an agreement of goals is established, they should be written clearly and concisely, and they should be distributed widely. The burden of fulfilling these goals should feel shared by a large part of the congregation.

It is not uncommon for a church to begin to collectively act to fulfill a goal once they have articulated it as something that genuinely will make a difference. In fact, I have seen churches regularly begin to implement some of their goals even before they have a chance to formally vote on them at a business meeting. The Cornerstone Church adult Sunday school class teachers readily understood how great it would be if each class would double in its average attendance. Before we could finish the planning process and present the final proposals for approval, two of the classes had already almost reached their goal of doubling in size.

Questions for conversation

- *What is going well in your church?*

- *What is not operating very effectively in your church?*

- *What changes have occurred in your community over the past 10 years?*

- *What new opportunities does your church need to consider embracing in the years to come?*

NOTES

WHAT BARRIERS CAN YOU EXPECT?

Change doesn't come easily to churches. We have been around for 2000 years, and in some cases we are very proud that we still do some of the same things the same way as it has always been done.

In fact, you might be among those in your congregation who get nervous whenever you hear others talking about how much needs to change. Churches can gain a new vision for the future and successfully pursue it.

The following story inspires me to hope for every church a brighter future. This story is transcribed from a video on the website of the Cottonwood Baptist Church in Dublin, Texas (www.cottonwoodtx.com).

In 1951, Amy Thackerson was one of a handful of members at this country church. She wrote, "We are about the same at Cottonwood. I guess it will never be anything but a spark. Never to become a bright shining light for God, though I have wished it could be for the last 30 years. Grandpa always had a longing that it could be great. Papa did, and I have hoped along with them that it might one day be something great. Grandpa silently sleeps there close by. Grandma, Momma, John, Mozella Morris and so many more that have had a part in keeping it sleep there also. I feel sometimes when I grow so very discouraged that they are calling me and telling me to never let go. But I pray that God's will may be done whatever that may be. I wonder what it would be like to go to another church. But I know I will never feel at home like I have ever felt at dear old Cottonwood. It would be like giving a loved one up for dead and trying to find another to take their place. It just couldn't be..."

The church fell on hard times. There was a group of four youth who attended the church by themselves and kept the doors open. They would sing some hymns, read the Scriptures, pray and collect an offering. One of the elderly women said, "I believe with all my heart, that in His time, God will reward the faithful few."

Today, the church averages around 700 in worship each Sunday, and is going on mission trips together with the missionaries they support all around the globe. This small country church made a firm decision when they called their new young seminary student as their next pastor that they would (1) love each other sincerely, and (2) obey the Lord. Together with this young pastor, they saw the hand of God bless the congregation in ways they never imagined.

Not every church experiences the touch of God like Cottonwood, but their hearts give us a powerful example to follow. Across the years, they determined to love each other and to obey God.

Change usually comes to churches very slowly. After more than 35 years of working in churches, I can attest to the fact that change will happen. It will just not happen after the pastor preaches one good message on the future direction of the congregation. I have to smile when I hear a new pastor express frustration over the fact that after preaching three times on a given topic, the people still aren't implementing it. For some reason, we have the expectation that once someone gives a clear direction, the congregation will immediately embrace the changes and begin acting in the different, prescribed way.

Very seldom do we experience change in our lives in that way. There are those among us who tend towards embracing change early on, and then there are others who will eventually join a change in direction once we are convinced it is a good change, and that it is indeed going to happen. Then there are others who resist change until it is absolutely forced upon them. They grudgingly leave the comfortable past, and complain and procrastinate all along the road to the future while wishing for the good old days.

What things should change? Our easy answer to this question is usually about things that are easy to change: the buildings, the programs, or even the budget. The deeper changes, however, are probably the ones we most need to consider when we look toward the future of our church. These are the changes in the habits of the people. How we do small groups. How we worship. How we prepare during the week for worship. How we relate to one another either at a superficial level or at a deeper, more intimate level.

As an organization, the church has developed a certain ethos that is more or less sacred. That ethos, or "the way we do things around here" may well have some terrible dysfunctions that go against the very teachings of Christ, and may quench the Spirit of God as He seeks to breathe new life into the body.

One congregation developed a culture that certain families, by their longevity of membership in the church, had veto power over every major decision made either by the pastor or the church body in a business meeting. This group not only felt entitled to quietly run the church from the background, but they freely warned anyone who dared to challenge them with a contrary plan that such an effort would never succeed as long as they were a part of this church. That small clique within the church has fired pastors and music ministers (without a church vote); squelched the approved long-range plan that the entire church had voted to affirm; and even nixed a pastoral candidate that the pastor search committee brought with a unanimous recommendation.

The more difficult things to talk about and then to change are the processes of making decisions, the manner in which a church deals with disagreements, and how the senior pastor leads. While this present work is not intended to be a manual on how to shift power and make change in a local church, it is a topic that I must touch upon in order to continue to my conclusion.

Unless a church is (1) aware of how it really makes decisions, and (2) is confident that this way of making decisions is the godliest and most workable way for that church at that time, it cannot consider adopting goals for a long range plan that will actually get implemented. To oversimplify this conversation, let me make three observations:

1. The size of the church will determine to some degree what type of power structure it has or needs. A small church of less than 60 can operate as a family with a single leader. Everyone has an opinion that matters on every issue, and together the whole family chooses the way (with the usual patriarch or matriarch in the mix). A mid-sized church will have some combination of committees and program leaders together with the pastor who really make the key decisions year after year. This could be called the church council model. The

larger churches become pastor and staff led, and the mega churches definitely invest an enormous amount of trust and power into the figure of the senior pastor. It is sometimes this dynamic that keeps a church from growing into a larger congregation. The family style church resists trusting power of decision to program leaders and staff. The committee-led church resists allowing a good pastor to actually lead.

2. The culture of a church determines how it expects to hear from God. In some cultures, the pastor is the only one who can authoritatively hear a word from God and then announce the direction of the church. In other cultures, the body is expected to pray, and in a very democratic way come up with a plan for going forward.

3. All models of church leadership should expect some resistance to change. The logic of this statement is something like this: Things are the way they are today for many reasons. Years of experience have led us to behave this way, organize ourselves this way, and to expect these kinds of results. In essence, today is the sum total of the recent history. An argument for change then must be more compelling than all of the reasons for the traditional processes. Policies have been placed in the records to prevent known past failures. A

policy manual usually comes into being one section at a time by the mistakes that are made in the church. If the youth minister messes up on a retreat, then a year later there will likely be a set of policies governing how youth retreats must be handled. A disaster involving a church van will result in a set of policies about van usage. In other words, churches write rules to prevent the mistake that just happened. Often these rules accumulate over the years into a massive wall of bureaucracy that prevents anything from getting done or anyone from changing anything. I served on the Missions Committee of a church that founded a new Hispanic Church across the street. I ended up taking the proposal for a new sign that would announce the name and services of the Hispanic Congregation through four different committees, and then before a general church business meeting before it could become reality. After six months of persistent work, we put up a sign announcing that we had started a new Spanish-speaking congregation. With less tenacity, it never would have happened. I don't retell this story for the purpose of bashing that church, but only to say that change will meet some very significant resistance before it eventually succeeds.

What are some of those barriers to change? Here is just a starter list. Your church can easily add more to the list.

- The church is content with the present reality.
- The church has tried things like this before and they always failed.
- This new project isn't in the budget.
- Someone (a key stakeholder) isn't going to like it.
- The great idea gets lost in the blur of busyness.
- A genuine disagreement about the vision. This barrier really goes back to embracing different sets of values.
- Goals are never clearly stated in the SMART form. In many cases, the goals fail to materialize because they don't belong to anyone in particular. They are orphaned without the responsible party picking up on it and owning it fully.

The list really has no end, because as long as someone proposes, someone else will oppose. That isn't a signal to give up, however, it is just a call to be realistic as you try to lead your church to talk about where it needs to go in order to be obedient to the head, Jesus Christ.

How does a group within the church get the rest of the church to move forward? How does it overcome the barriers erected to stop such movement?

The first advice that I would give any group comes from something I heard my own father say repeatedly: "Be Christian." In whatever conflict we find ourselves, we can hear and respond to the voice of Him whom we call Lord. He commanded forgiveness, love, perseverance, and faith. He called us to pray persistently. He urged us to go out trusting Him to provide for our needs.

The Apostle Paul also added a great checklist in Romans 12:9-21. We don't overcome resistance to change the same way the world does. That is because we see our fellow church members as parts of the Body. We are slow to attack another part of the body of Christ because we know that we too will be held accountable for all we say and do to either destroy it or to build it up.

Since change takes time, we must be patient and trust that it will come.

It also helps to show our brothers and sisters what needs to change and why it needs to change through a new set of eyes. One simple example of this is to invite an important outsider to come in and take a tour of the entire church facility. Have a group of those who think everything is just fine accompany this outsider and look at things through their eyes. Suddenly, the moldy smelly bathroom becomes an embarrassment instead of "good enough." The "secret guest" kind of approach might help as well. This is where the congregation invites unknown guests to come and participate in their services at an unannounced time, and then send back their opinions through a questionnaire.

Another approach is to send groups from your church to visit loved and respected congregations during their key service times and come back and make a report of their impressions. The approach that is taken to produce a desire to change is different for each congregation. The one thing that is very consistent is that energy, effort, and time must be spent on producing that desire for change. It will not be self-evident, and it will not happen without effort.

A cursory browsing of world languages and cultures reveals a funny human tendency: to not take plans and words very seriously. Spanish speakers joke that everything will happen "mañana." A translation of a favorite Indonesian proverb is "Things take longer than they take." Arabic speakers often use the phrase, "insha'allah" (if Allah wills it) as they finish stating something about the future that probably won't happen... or at least not very soon. Like, "I will come back and pay you the rest of the money soon, "insha'allah."

Churches use the phrase, "Let's give that to the committee to look into it and bring back a report" to delay actually doing something about issues that seem complex or too difficult to tackle. There is certainly wisdom in allowing a committee some extra time to deliberate the details of a plan, but there is often a laziness that underlies these decisions that would be embarrassing if it were spoken out loud.

A church needs to keep listening to the different members of the body, but it cannot allow a small group to hold the whole body hostage to implied threats or intimidation. The real question before the congregation is not "What do I want?" but "What does the Lord want?" The wrong question to ask is "How can I get my way?" Instead, ask "How can we more effectively accomplish our mission, remain loyal to our values, and become the church we are called to be?"

The concept of consensus is helpful here. So is prayer. So is mutual submission.

Questions for conversation

• *What obstacles have you already faced when trying to help your church become healthier?*

• *Who might oppose any planning process that might bring about significant changes?*

• *When was the last time your congregation made a major change in its ministry, schedule, or programming?*

NOTES

WHY SHOULD YOU PERSEVERE?

The church really matters. It is the bride of Christ. It is the light of the world. It is the hope of any community. It is worth the effort! There is no other alternative.

As the disciples were made aware of the thousands of deserters, Jesus asked them, "Will you leave too?" Their response speaks to our current theme: "Only you have the words of life." If we give up on the church, what are we going to invest our lives in that will make any difference? I am aware that many non-profits are doing much good, but none of them have the same mission—to make disciples.

Without perseverance, nothing changes. If a new ministry is worth launching, then it will take considerable sweat equity, money, and time.

Hay Valley in Gatesville was founded in the late 1800's. Since it is located in a rural county in Texas, the population around the church hasn't changed dramatically in its entire history. It has seen days when the average attendance touched 100, and other years when it sank to the low 30s.

A local businessman and his family decided to invest in their church. When I visited with them, they were very discouraged. They had called a pastor with a very high sense of moral authority. In brief, the pastor was always right. Through the course of about three years, he bumped heads with family after family over petty issues. Many families left, but the core families of the church hung together. They did not become combative, but simply insisted on doing things in a decent and orderly way.

Finally the pastor grew tired of their steadfast resistance, and moved on to start his own church a few miles away. They have, through the years, weathered some really good times and some really bad times. Their commitment to their church has not faltered. These families are looking way beyond today into tomorrow when their grandchildren will be able to learn the stories about Jesus within the walls of this same church.

What happens when a church cannot find renewal and live again?

While a church has a natural life-cycle, every community needs a good church. That means that as long as there is a community of people living together, there is a need for a gathering place for believers who are seeking to follow Jesus together.

As the community transitions so must the church. Communities change in many different ways, but primarily by who lives there. These changes can be very challenging for a church because they are profound in the ways people live, communicate, celebrate, and collaborate. Changes in language, culture, income levels, and generations all bring significantly different ways of doing things. For many churches, these differences become too large and the church, in effect, sits isolated and insulated from the community until it dies.

Over the past several years I have had the blessing of walking with these churches through their end-of-life decisions. In many cases, we have been able to find a new, growing, and culturally relevant church to come and take over the facilities of the older congregation that had lived out its years of good ministry with dignity and grace. In each case, the remaining members have yearned for the Good News of Jesus to carry on. And if possible, they wanted their investments in their facilities to be used for the furtherance of the Gospel. Selflessly and generously, they have handed their remaining assets over to the new growing congregation with a blessing and a prayer.

My only wish, in most of these cases, was that this graceful transition could have happened a little sooner. The older dying congregation held on to their giant facilities (which they could no longer maintain adequately) way beyond a reasonable time, and as a result, the facilities suffered sad deterioration that almost rendered them useless to anyone who would follow. They let leaky roofs accumulate moisture and water in the walls to the point that mold prevented the building from ever being used again. They allowed the broken windows and vandalism to remain unrepaired until the facility really needed to be torn down. What could have been a blessing ends up being just an eye sore in the neighborhood.

When we speak of "Why should you persevere?" we might need to understand that in some cases perseverance means facing reality and making good courageous decisions while some good can come from it.

Questions for conversation

- *What will likely be the consequence of you doing nothing about the future of your church?*

- *Who will you have in mind while you are patiently investing your energies, time and prayers into the future of your church?*

- *How do you keep fresh spiritually while your church undergoes discomfort or transition?*

- *How is the church different from a retail business in your community?*

- *How would you know if your church has come to the end of its life and needs to plan the ending so that the Gospel can go forward?*

NOTES

WHAT ELSE MUST YOU CONSIDER?

Is the current pastoral leadership called, capable, and competent to lead your church?

This is the most painful chapter for me to write as I reflect on my years of experience with churches. I have come to the conclusion that some pastors who occupy the position of a pastor in a church should not be there. I have seen churches err on both sides of this problem. As it becomes evident that a pastor is not the right one to lead a congregation, some churches have simply sat on that knowledge and allowed the pastor to either blow the church to pieces or to wait until the church sleepily slides into oblivion. I have also seen church leaders jump on a campaign to fire a pastor and, because of their imprudence or impatience they themselves blow the church to pieces.

I am writing intentionally to a tradition where the congregation is the only entity that has the authority to place or remove the pastor. Most other Christian denominations have a hierarchy of bishops or district presidents that can intervene and solve this dilemma for the local congregation. The advice I offered in the previous chapter applies here as well. You might want to go back and reread that chapter if this is a point you are seriously considering for your church.

I really tried to avoid writing on this topic in this small book, but as I reflected on my experiences with many congregations over the years, I realized that it is this one topic that (1) lacks clear guidelines in our churches, and (2) has the potential to ruin our churches more than perhaps any other thing I have mentioned in the previous chapters. The mishandling of the issue of pastoral leadership can result in real conflict, confusion, and even the demise of the local church.

When a congregation realizes that the current pastor is not really suited for leading them into the future, the best scenario for a change is obviously a negotiated, patient, peaceful transition. As the church tries to "be Christian" in their approach to the pastor, so the pastor should "be Christian" in his or her dealings with the church.

When I wrote this chapter, I assumed that entire books existed on how to properly fire a pastor. I found none. There are paragraphs or chapters within other books that address this issue, but I haven't discovered one that is definitive on this topic. Most church bylaws spell out some bit of a process the church can go through in order to let their pastor go. Most of the governing documents of the churches name a committee or a group (deacons or elders) who should handle this issue when it turns negative. Naming that group, however, doesn't solve the problem of how to make the process as fair and helpful as possible for all of the stakeholders involved.

I believe that most of the church bylaws and constitutions omit several key resources that could make a pastor's termination more peaceful and fair:

- The help of an outside mediator.
- The naming of important benchmarks along in the process including what is considered a reasonable time frame for each step, and what happens if that timeframe is exceeded.
- The listing of important denominational resources that can facilitate a smoother transition for all involved.
- A listing of the most relevant passages of Scripture that speak directly to the issue of holding leaders accountable, challenging leaders when they fall, and redeeming leaders who have failed.

Here is the sad bottom line in some cases: the church will not survive or move forward as long as the current pastor is in that position. If this is the case for your congregation, then the painful conversations and changes are important for the sake of the Gospel.

For good insights into the relationship between a pastor and congregation, I would recommend the book, Pastor and People: Making Mutual Ministry Work by Richard J. Brueschoff, 2003, Augsburg Fortress.

The First Baptist Church had enjoyed the pastoral leadership of Bro. Bob for almost 20 years. He had married and buried and baptized many of the members of the congregation. Although the church had endured several significant "leavings" of groups of families through the years, Bob continued ministering faithfully, and maintained the trust of the majority of the congregation.

The effectiveness of Bob's leadership, however seemed to diminish through years 15 -20. These last five years were characterized by persistent conflict with staff, downward trends in every measure of the church life, expressions of frustration and disillusionment, and the inability to propose and carry out effectively any new initiatives.

As Bob became concerned about his own effectiveness, he sought wise outside counsel from fellow pastors and denominational leaders. Through a period of six months Bob realized that his time of effective ministry at First Baptist Church was really over. With the help of trusted outsiders, he negotiated a salary and benefits package that would (1) allow him a reasonable time to seek another ministry position elsewhere; (2) give the church a specific and definitive date when he would be resigning; and (3) allow all of his supporters and friends the opportunity to bless him and encourage him as he left on a good note. Neither the church nor the pastor was destroyed in what could have been a devastating transition.

Questions for conversation

- *How painful is the topic of this chapter to you personally?*

- *What do you need to communicate to your church leader-ship in light of this chapter?*

- *Who do you need to enlist to pray together with you about the thoughts that have come into your mind while you have read this booklet?*

NOTES

THE AUTHOR

Tim Randolph is the Director of the Waco Regional Baptist Association in Waco, Texas. He has been involved in Baptist church life all of his life. His parents served in a variety of mission and church capacities throughout their careers, and Tim began preaching at the age of 15. He has served as a pastor, church planter, international missionary, and a Director for Baptist Associations during his 36 years of service. His long experience in church and denominational life has equipped Tim with a unique insight into how churches are born, grow, change, and then in some cases die. His passion for the local church has driven him to study, experiment, and try different approaches to helping churches find their focus, passion, and mission within their specific context.

Tim's wife, Cindy, and their children have been longtime participants in the churches and ministries in which Tim has been engaged. Tim enjoys the outdoors by cycling, hiking, swimming, and running.